Books by George Quasha

FIVE BLIND MEN
AMANITA'S HYMNAL
MAGIC SPELL FOR THE FAR JOURNEY
SOMAPOETICS (BOOK ONE)
WORD YUM (SOMAPOETICS 64-69)
GIVING THE LILY BACK HER HANDS
AINU DREAMS
IN NO TIME

as editor/co-editor

STONY BROOK
OPEN POETRY
AMERICA A PROPHECY
ACTIVE ANTHOLOGY
THE STATION HILL BLANCHOT READER

as co-author

HAND HEARD/LIMINAL OBJECTS
TALL SHIPS
VIEWER

Ainu Dreams

poems
George Quasha

in collaboration with
Chie [buun] Hasegawa

STATION HILL
BARRYTOWN, LTD.

Published by Station Hill / Barrytown, Ltd.
in Barrytown, NY 12507.

E-mail: publishers@stationhill.org
Online catalogue: http://www.stationhill.org

Station Hill Arts is a project of The Institute for Publishing Arts, Inc., a not-
for-profit, tax-exempt organization in Barrytown, New York, which grate-
fully acknowledges ongoing support for its publishing program from the
New York State Council on the Arts.

Drawings by George Quasha.

Calligraphy on page 1—"Ma"—and page 144—"Tamashi"—are from the
marvelous Cooper-Hewitt Museum catalogue [n.d.] (for the "Ma" exhibi-
tion, with architect Arata Isozaki), editor: Seigow Matsuoka; artist: Shiro
Kuramata; et al. Reproduced with gratitude and admiration. See our
"Afterwords" for brief discussion of these rich terms.

Special thanks to Gail Dennis of Chadmark Farms in Paso Robles, Califor-
nia, for generously supplying the pomegranate (out of season and on short
notice) used in the cover photo.

Further acknowledgement in the colophon.

Library of Congress Cataloging-in-Publication Data

Quasha, George.
 Ainu dreams : poems / George Quasha in collaboration with Chie
(buun) Hasegawa.
  p. cm.
 ISBN 1-58177-053-7 (alk. paper)
 1. Dreams Poetry. I. Hasegawa, Chie buun. II. Title.
PS3567.U28A73 1999
811'.54—dc21
                                                                99-23226
                                                                    CIP

Manufactured in the United States of America.

in the spirit of recognizing our sources
we dedicate this work to

CHOEGYAL NAMKHAI NORBU

and to our mothers

ARVIE

&

CHINAE

CONTENTS

Afterwords

A Word Before

something like the facts of the matter

Ainu Dreams is a collaborative work begun in 1994, and this first book comprises some eighty poems. Beyond this volume the work continues without a concept of ending. The poems are based entirely on the dreams of Chie Hasegawa, a Japanese artist living in America for more than a decade, who prefers the *nom be plume* buun (and writes it in minuscule). I have written the poems in active collaboration with her, the dreamer, who was most often physically present during much of the writing process and exerted a continuous, sharp and uncompromising corrective force on the composition. The poems are deeply faithful to the dreams and preserve their actual content, and even in various ways the language of the dreamer. At the same time, *Ainu Dreams* is a work inside poetry and develops according to the inner necessity of the poem itself and by a *metapoetic* principle: that each poem embodies an originary poetics, unique to its own possibility. How it could be that I declare this process of poetry as belonging to "my" work is both something quite clearly known to me and a mystery of poetry that informs in the nature of poetry—that this "my" is in no way exclusive of "our" or, to be sure, "her." Something of this complex matter finds its expression in "Oneiropoeia—Telling Tales on Dreaming" at the end of the book.

Of the hundreds of extraordinary dreams that buun recorded at my request—many written in a notebook, either in English or Japanese or a combination of both, and many spoken into a tape recorder and later transcribed—the ones that made it to these pages are those in which, in our view, the dreaming process and the writing process fully merged. There is a voice, an identity, inside each poem that determines its own course. It is at one level always *the voice of a woman dreaming*, although sometimes it announces itself as male. These are, in a sense, "dramatic" facts. Yet in becoming the voice of the poem, the dream goes beyond the identity of the actual dreaming person, and even *beyond gender*. In a certain sense the identities of both dreamer and poet have left their ordinary seats in the "actual" persons and *joined*—perhaps in something like the ancient sense of *alchemical wedding*—in a new identity that is larger than "person," except in the root sense of *sounding through*.

My companion in these poems says she found her way to a new "identity" rooted in dream and poetry and expressed in the name "buun" which announced itself in the process and stands complexly in dialogue with "Chie." This dialogue of names/identities somehow reflects a non-ordinary ambidexterity indirectly thematized in the dreams. buun values the optimal miniature and a guardian modesty of intimate space; Chie carries forward the ancestors and the force of public space; etc. She is now further "twinning" this process by taking *Ainu Dreams* into Japanese, creating both a translation and a new original. This complication of the question of "what is the original"—like its correlative "who is the author"—is intrinsic to this work, as it seems to be in one way or another to poetry itself.

For my part I have found in the process of this composition further confirmation of a lifelong view—namely, that the poem has a source *outside* personal boundaries, even when a poem is driven by what seems most personal. I understand the poet's role as maintaining a discipline of listening to a specific source, in this case situated at once in the dream and in emerging language. Poetry in my view is first of all *speaking with listening*—a peculiar state that is somehow self-optimizing, somehow self-awakening.

I could say a lot about what this process has meant to me, but in many ways it comes down to gratitude. It would strain the performative value of language to attempt to express that gratitude, beyond thanking my companion in the work for her willingness to stay with it. Nevertheless I want to extend the emphasis on *listening*, beyond its core role as stance in the radical of composition, to include the actual listeners/readers whose energetic attendance contributes to the emerging work. First of all my two other close companions in poetry, art and life, Susan Quasha and Charles Stein, offer listening at the heart of poetic possibility itself. About them it could be said:

> Hearing them hearing the poem
> teaches the poem to hear itself.

Ontononymous the Particular

Along similar lines I wish to thank the many people who listened to these poems as they were written and "fed us back," including Linda Weintraub and Raquel Rabinovich, who also organized the Rhinebeck *peñas* where over a few years many of the poems were read each month to friends. Beyond this, we find ourselves thanking Dream and Poetry and their protectors and inhabitants—but the permissions of this occasion may not extend that far, at least not in the voice of anything like *the facts of the matter.*

GQ, Barrytown, New York, September 1998 / February 1999

Ainu Dreams

The Fool

in black
misfit tights
came up to me and said
everything is one half
comedy
and one half
comedy
and handed me
with his two hands
his two
heads

New Year's Day

I wanted to fly a kite
but I couldn't find the sky

Nest Living

At the top of this
tall, leafless tree,
crutched in the bare branches,
there's a nest, and I
and my big bird call it home.
I myself am a bird
from the waist down.

Our mostly white but partly blue feathers
cover the nest quite comfortably,
and we are warming a blue-green egg.
He—the bird, my husband—does it a while
and then I do it a while.
I am happy. I feel responsible.
We are collaborating beautifully.

I Am a Member of the Mind Circus

My job is to sell a certain number of tickets.
Problem is, there are conditions:
Not just anyone can come.
You have to be in a particular state of mind
even to get past the door.
So I'm out tracking down the self-chosen
yet can't seem to lay my hands on 'em. Stuck!

(In the background we're doing *the practice of color*.)

On the other hand, I have an elephant friend.
We're close.
He sticks with me through thick and thin.
And right now the performance is about to happen,
indeed the audience is getting excited.
There's a rumor afoot:

Da Vinci is coming!

The rest is history.

Age of Wings

My nape slit open
by itself
and out came two trans-
     parent wings,
          these dragonfly look-alikes.

A weird place to have wings,
and it's been worrying me to even think
about using them...

A man at the threshold speaks out to me,
    Take good care of them, they'll grow
    and change, and slowly change color.

These wings deserve close attention
like fine lace, each little section
originating its own pattern, latticing
its own life, turning into sounds
slightly willing to communicate.

Now the man takes out his eerie tool
to measure the scope of a wing:

    It's three circles old.

I Get Reversed

Inside
is coming
outside.

Can't recall
how it happens.

Everything around me
is reversed.

Must have *done* something but can't remember what.
Try not to get confused or lost:
Which is inside,
which is outside.

I start peeling
from the sexual part
like undressing, folding back
the inside out, slowly.

Where is my center now?
Try to remain, by all means, in myself.
Consider an outside possibility—
to be openminded.

Which can only mean *everything inside
revealed.* Sucked in
or out. Anyway, *pulled.*

Anxiously trying to get a handle on how it happened—
the verse, the order—What is First—
left arm, say—so as to be able, later,
to return.

To reverse
one last time.

Journeying

Lying on my back, this
long, long hair of mine
flows behind me
and becomes a road
leading to a huge and special place.
This is the only possible way to get there.

So people start walking, heading out
on my hair, on the lengthening journey along the road....

And I warn them to take off their shoes.
Yet, incredibly, some just keep on walking.
I start to get angry, sorry
I ever invited them at all.
Still, I realize that I alone
am responsible for getting them there.

Meanwhile people are arriving
and already they have begun to do this
very particular body movement
which can only be done in a certain state.

And one by one they disappear.

Instrumental Opening

"Promise me," you were saying
on your way out the door, "you'll find it,
the instrument for you and you alone,"
and you quickly handed me an old catalogue.
Almost everything made no sense—
the words, the numbers, with only
an occasional exception (e.g., Yamaha)—yet
eventually I came upon the very one, lo!

It comes from Iceland!

And even now it's reaching straight into my hands.

I learn right away the very particular conditions
for playing this instrument—

Specifications:

It has to be cold—a ¼ freezing state,
and the wind's got to be something-something
(and much much more), and
if you blow some air into the hole (just a little
is enough to loosen the joints) it's not too stiff—

Whereupon a core strategic discovery—

you can unfold it!

I do, and naturally it ends up

eighteen feet across,
rounded and so finely pared
the supple skin conveys the light,
with openings all around....

Now I get it—
this is an instrument for *many mouths
breathing in time,*

joining
limb to spine, body to body,
intimately tuning the
hidden one
through the one opening

in the middle

waiting for the single

sound to come

Rebound

Lying longer than planned on the couch
stretch my arms
way out
and stretch and stretch and
even stretch some more
only to bounce
back

It's really quite upsetting
to come all the way back in
only to find one's very own body
altogether
changed

I Am the Master Box Maker

I hold out my hand
with a perfect little box—

    Lines shoot out from the corners
                in perspective

          and a thin light line creates
          a box of new proportions

and a transparent hand holds it
and a body transparent under it

and the intelligent lines go out
and thread power-
                fully into a box, another
          left hand, a connecting body, and

live a further life, a fine
attenuated enclosure
in filaments, shooting out
                toward some *other...*

—But wait, from where I stand, it's quite clear now
          there are still more
              reaching dimensions
                    lining up in the line of sight...

I Was Designing a Human Airplane

like this:
      Lying down
      on white paper,
      arms raised above my head,
      writing in blue pen
      the sizes and proportions
      —wings, tail, etc.—
      according to the parts of my own body.

And of course whatever you write down
that's what you have to be.

      I am closing my eyes now and
      waiting
                yet still
             stretching out here
                completing the design to the point of
           inscribing when

    it ignites within
           the unpotentiated paper
               the absorbable power
                        to fly

I Am Looking

for a house
to live in
near the graveyard
of my ancestors

with you, still

Healing Ritual

It's my grandfather
on my mother's side

With my left hand
I hold his penis

and I dip it
in a beaker
in the liquid
the color of milk tea

and it catches fire

There Are Places

where you can still see the ancestors

here and there
the leftovers, the strays

When reflecting on them, finding myself
        thinking it's up to me to
            gather them together...

                        a voice slices the air—

                It is not
            a matter of
    consolidating ancestors

like soup

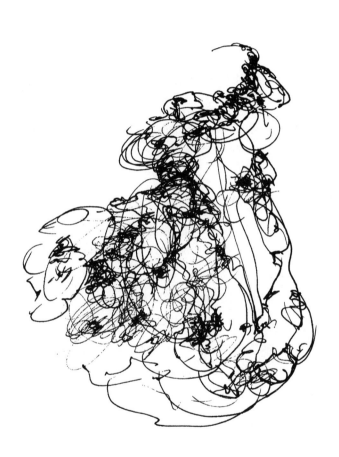

Changing Form

I was riding my bike, minding my own business
and heading out toward the Shingon temple

when I felt some force coming upon me, taking me
under, setting my wheels spinning through the sky.

Autumn leaves
came out of my mouth.

Cops appeared, wasting no time in fingering *me*
—two grabbed me by the arms to haul me off.

"I was just on my way to the temple," I tried to explain,
but they weren't listening. These guys

really want to hurt me. Not mere change,
mutation!—Lawman

metamorphs into *monster!*—No escape: *This
is a dream dreaming*

itself! Imperative
now to use all will to convert miscreation to

you.
Translation before my eyes

into many, many luminous spots—
flowing particular light enters into my body

and still I'm getting this eerie, dispiriting feeling
all too familiar

in dreams of the kind, nightmare neighbors.
So this is it, the sign

of failure in turning
the willful monstrous

into my own best
other—you, still, somehow with me.

Department Store

Closeout sale!
Yes, and there's hardly anything left.
I fix on a fierce mask—
the kind called *Prajna* where I come from—
two horns, gold teeth, earthen complexion,
fangs sticking way out....
Frankly, I'm not really wild about the face
—feels worn out, and listless.

> *(My father once said, "The Prajna mask*
> *is a woman*
> *in a state of ecstasy."*
> *My mother replied, "How do you know that?"*
> *And my father, "It's obvious.")*

So I ask the salesperson,
"Is there nothing more here
howling from the deeps?"

Apple

I am an apple.

Someone comes along and cuts off a piece.
Terrible, I'll go rotten!

Instantly
I regenerate.

Oh
it's good I can do that.

Risqué

We are roses,
the three of us,
red, white, and rosé—
which is which is unclear
but it doesn't really matter.

Who's the riskiest of them all?
She slopes her wavy stem to lift
her slip and let show—flesh
out—forbidden root
rousing, achingly outenduring us all.

Knot

I was a knot,
or else, I was inside a knot.

Not sure.

Here's the story: I was making a knot
with myself.

Out of the blue someone asks: *What's it like
to be inside a knot?*

I say: I was the knot itself,
or the knot could have been in me or, well,
maybe, after all, I may have slipped into the knot.

*When you became the knot
where were you? Is mind inside
or out?*

Hang on, we're losing the thread.
As sides go, there's no in or out here.
Once a knot, there's only
this side.

Philosophical Immunity

I was in the closet
and realized that someone
was trying to stick
needles in my skin.

So I decided to gather together
the complete works of Socrates
and wear them
as armor.

Now no one can get to me.
Suddenly the idea comes into my head
that I should be doing the exact same thing
with Nietzsche and Sartre.

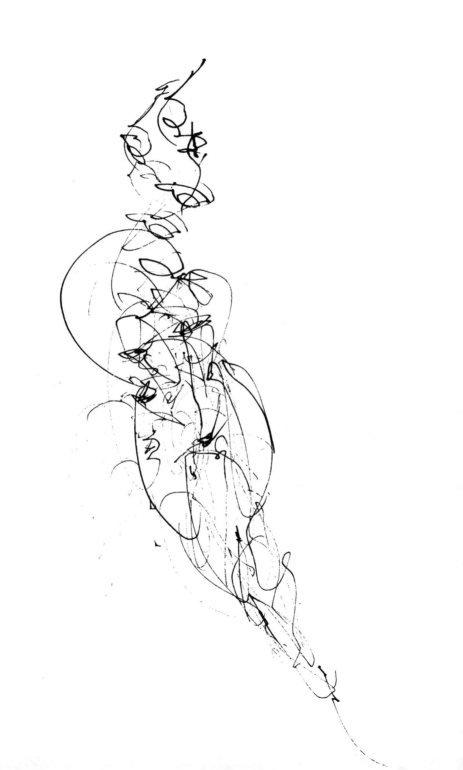

A Woman Is Carrying the Full Moon

in slices

Seems random,
yet each cut serves precisely
to protect her.

This light-bearing mass
looks familiar,
so I ask,

"Is this moon from last night?"

"No," she says, "It's from
six months ago."

Big Moon on the Verge

of touching down

grounding in the bright snow all around

yet bounding within reach

And all night long I'm haunted by the thought—
Somehow I ought to be able to store this phenomenon in my computer—
bodily processing the whole surrounding view:

snowed-in earth piled high enough
to embrace the surrendering
luminous globe
or
the great ball alighting at last

Or else somewhere in between —
here? where am I? how high
the sky?

WORKING THE IDEOGRAM UP
INTO MOTION

I burst into laughter
—intimate with snow and levitating communion—
squeezing in right here between lip and
crux of grand bodies

Being Partial

I was a man
and I was trying to save a woman in danger.

I picked her up in my arms
and flew.

Flying like a frog swimming in air
I ditched our nameless pursuer

and landed. There was a guy
waiting for us

who looked
like a king.

Caught.
Now I have to accept the punishment

for saving the woman.
First,

we have to take a shower.
The effect is to loosen

the skin from the muscle
until it peels off.

The woman
picks up the pieces of my skin and

holds them in her hands
and says: *I will love each of these*

as I loved you.
And I thought: This is what is called

Fetish. And suddenly it came to me that the origin
of the word is *fe-* as in *female*, soft, loving, silken —

plus *-tissue.* Like tissues flying.
Voicing particles waking in waves

over a living body
of water

loose at last

Communication

Playing catch
with a huge round stone,
enjoying it!
but still can't believe we're
actually doing it—

tight-rope tension
in the game, stretching out
the anger in the air—yet
suspending emotion

it's so precise
breathing . . . timing
the focus, the aim
charged with danger

—the stone
is bigger than my body!

Attention slacks, a
missing moment, I
lose
presence
and you are ruthless
in maintaining the tension
across this split second
hurling the stone to the center of my body

I receive it
right here,
here at the core
—the weight, I
feel it now and
the pain, the loss, the
break at the root of the
spell

Two Objects Hanging in Air

ONE ROUND, ANOTHER
ELONGATED
APPEAR
TO BE MADE
OF ANIMAL HIDE

AND HOLLOW
WITH DRUM-HEAD TRANSLUCENCE

Seeing these playable objects I sense
they configure here to serve as

power spot

and apparently from time to time
you're supposed to go up
and touch them.

Ready? Let's start the ceremony.
Good thing for both of us I remember learning
how to be in the perfect state
required to perform this rite.
Still, I can't help reflecting
on the question in your mind—
what makes it perfect?

feeling
light

And what can this mean but *weightless and free,* and the whole
touching room is flooding

lightwise

Carriers

Together at the long table,
you were right next to me
writing a letter to a poet friend, whereupon

he appeared!
right there, between us—

physically
or not.

No doubt you could say it either way and it would be
as true.
He was there.

This made me want to write to him as well,
thinking, *I too can make a magical thing like that happen.*

So I started writing.

Wherefore the following result: the poet
became a soft lavender.
The shape of the body was unchanged, but the rest was color,
pure pervasive lavender.
And a stream of this color was going out
and entering deeply into *you.*

Either he was projecting it
or you were sucking it in.
No way to be sure about such things, yet
I can't resist saying,

The truth words carry power.

You had the ability, right there next to me,
to raise the words
                    like the dead
awakening
to the life still hiding inside them.
And more and more you embodied the lavender.

The question nevertheless presses on: Did I
or did you
actually do it?

Twins at Hand

So here we are at the big wedding
but I don't know *whose.*
This little gathering in the waiting room
is to get the protocol, and there, in the middle,
our Teacher is starting to instruct us.
He performs a series of gestures and
oh god, worst fear, they're *boring!*
Not-to-be-believed politician-hype in mannered clichés,
here executed with the high-minded seriousness of
sacred *mudra.*
I protest.
Can't hold back the truth —

                      these are the gestures
that make me sick. And I say so.

"Well," our Teacher responds,
"you have to understand the difference—
this isn't a matter of *two-handed peace signs.*"
The others boldly take *my* side, and
I proclaim that I certainly will not
do anything of that nature at the wedding.

"*This,*" I say, "is the only gesture *I'll* make":

        I signal from the heart, a flick of the wrist
            and quick, light, lifting palm face-up
                —spare as a magician's white-glove release
                      of a pigeon in the air—

in a flash my own *mudra* of

Heart Firing

Two
hearts appear
at once
suspended above my hand

flaring

—and a sudden clarity—

this is
his action,
my space

A Logic of Two Kinds

There are two kinds of people:
those who catch
and those who pitch.
Then there are those who hit.
I remember you said
there are two kinds of people:
those who can catch
and those who can't.
I catch.
So I decided to become
one who hits.

Two Arts

One
looks through the eye
in the middle.

And the other
idea says

Don't think
eyes
or any other funny language thing
for that matter.

Two Cars Parked in the Parking Lot

One green, one white...

I know,
I lived in New York!

This Much

Jonathan: "Can I have
a lot of opinions, please?"

I replied: "Cut down 25%."

What's it like to be 84%?

Even more to the point,
What's the relationship of the skin to the bones?

These among the many questions appearing vertical
turn one
by one

into

rain

A fat man comes along and cynically observes,
"All these questions are therefore the same."

I get irritated
and show the two maroon hats of my friend,

"I bet you think these are the same too!"

Around & About Tibet

A perfectly round lake
surrounded by an old, small village
suddenly starts to turn
around and around
and the small, old village inevitably
turns with it.
I realize it's a dream and

This is the famous
Roulette Lake

Traveling Around in Southern Caucasia

In Georgia I found a round typewriter.
And as I put my fingers to the keys
the world around me started to turn.
Some things turned upon themselves,
some things spun in full surround.

But that's the past, or maybe
it's somewhere else around here.
And now I'm sitting in this cafe,
windows all around me,
dining upon some strange
sweet Georgian cooking,
ready to tell what I came here to tell:
how I'd found a round typewriter
and things'd begun to spin around me..
when the woman beside me begins her tale
of how things started spinning around her,
and I cry out, "Why? Why
are you saying this, why are you telling my story?"
Out of nowhere a policeman appears,
and it's me he wants to arrest.
It seems I'm guilty of shoplifting
one round typewriter and a Georgian sweet.
I bribe him.
And as he turns to go, he mentions:
"Careful in Georgia!
You can shoplift here to your heart's content
except for two vitally important items:
the famous Georgian sweet on your plate
and the round typewriter at your fingertips."

Meaningless Chili

is what they called this thing
I was eating.
All the while the thought was running through my mind,
Just by continuing to eat, everything
will turn into meaninglessness!

It dawned on me, this isn't my thought, this is *them* speaking.
In fact, I ate a whole bowl
but absolutely nothing happened.

I complained:
How come I still have this emotion?
Still feel kind of sad.
So I ordered another bowl.

The guy who served, however, urged me
to wait a while, there were complications, words
to the effect,

> *This is the wrong thing*
> *for the wrong person.*

The tablecloth was white
but in the middle, a big black hole
in place of a serving bowl.

Here the guy gave even more explicit direction,

> *Feed the rest of the chili to the hole.*

While he spoke the white bowl covered over
the black hole, prominently invisible.

Now I see the bowl
has disappeared.

Come to think of it, all along I couldn't escape the impression
that the guy serving the food had come
from the hole.

He too has slipped from view.

Phone Call

It's for you

from Blink Your Eye

Do you believe it?

I *will* believe! However,

if I do actually manage to talk with him
I'll have to become a bit less concrete
due to the fact he's so incredibly abstract

—that is, not so bound to the human
as I.

      So, before saying hello,
I try my level best to deconcretize (not,
mind you, dematerialize,
which would be impressive but
beside the point)
           and I take my effort as a sign
that I'm getting close to ready
           —I mean

I can't exactly become a drop of water
just to be able to talk to him....

Oh the other hand, I can make believe.

Telling Sky

The woman called Everyday Goddess and I
have been watching the stars in the sky,

lying stretched out on the ground,
whereupon the stars start

moving—complexly—
continuously making

self-changing sculptural forms,
some coming close to us, some

drifting away: 3-D movie
The Sky all over us, "Wow!"

we rejoin to the moving
news clearing the mind, "All

the stars in the sky are
one being."

☞

We go in the house with the people. A woman
showing instruments she made fingers a flute

of big autumn leaves rolled up,
of hinted colors and low brightness,

wabi and *sabi,* scarce, sparse, lonely, sad, essential
things only. She starts playing, a

person in the room puts
her hand on her heart

and pronounces a strange word.
Stranger yet, everybody there understands:

O my heart, suddenly clear, spoken in Ultimate,
the language known only

to any-
one present

Flying Doctor

Flying doctor in a small village
I was
And busy, busy
Treating the sick
I was, I was
Very, very busy
And quite, quite exhausted.

And so it was that I came to the decisive point
That I should start walking
And so I walked and walked and
Took to standing on my head and walking.
And it came to my mind that this can only be
Because I am a crab. And I thought: A crab
Does this, walks like this. I am
A very busy crab, and very
Very exhausted.

And so it happened that my exhaustion reached the point
Of being obvious to others, so obvious
That they turned the tables on me and
The examination fixed
On me, on me
The doctor, the barely walking doctor,
And someone came, came to examine,
To examine my chest.
And he almost didn't want to see my chest
Because he was afraid to.
Who was he? Afraid of what?
And I hunkered down.

2

So heavy.
I'm so heavy.
It's spoiling the joy of flying.
But I keep on going
Until I fly across a place so huge
It's got to be a country fair.
I land.
Looks like everyone knows me,
Everyone is turning
Toward me
With heartfelt greetings,
In celebration of good deeds done.
They know me, it turns out,
Because I helped a lesbian couple
Untangle their hearts.
Actual physical untanglement.

The hat seller offers the gift of a hat.
She picks the one with the rubbery rim
You can pull down all the way
To cover your ears.

Flying Upward

almost
vertically
        and higher and higher
        deep inside the layering cloud cumulus

This is the highest I've ever been!

In a matter of time
I land.
       Men
are returning from the war,
their families are here to pick them up.
A motherless boy of seven is here alone
to find his father. In time
they reunite. Still, he cries
desperately. He misses his stuffed bear
just now lost, his animal being, his Mary,
still feeling his mother there, calling
her, pursuing her, con-
fusing longing, lingering loss, and moving

me inside, making me extend
my hand, spontaneous instinct
and sudden merged intention—me, mother, Mary
manifest

highest in the sky

Mary, herself, her vertical lightning nature
in optimal focused descent

straight to him, his arms, receiving,
hold open

Human Paint

I was out and about when I found my way
into the state
of paint

like happening to cut the bounding line of
color itself, my
self exposure
                    panoramic
                        space
fills up—
color abounds,
in turn spills over—
it looks
just-painted, wet
and yet more
flesh than paint, my own
color-breathing body painting un-
limited landscape,
just born, bound
to claim a tincture of the
moment itself
back around to me

Odds Are

I accidentally found an invisible door, and lo!
it lifted right out of the front of my body!

You open this door by sheer intention
and suddenly your garbage—
                              your past
and all its old emotions—
                              empties out.
But it only lasts a split second and
then as fast as it all began I
fill up with the garbage again
flowing back in through the self-same opening
in a flash.
                Can't seem to slam it shut in time.

At this moment Fontaine comes in,
starts to tell me how I really have to know
how much he loves me—
it's absolutely required for a Ph.D.
Instinctively I realize, if only
I could be
touched in that empty interim
I would *know*.
"No doubt about it."
So I try.
Now my heart is totally open
—I feel it *burning*—and
in that spaceless infinitesimal space I
try again and again and again to
beat the odds
                and slam the door in time....

Openness under pressure!

                       And, still, a certain joy
in the possibility...
                 And when he says, "I love you," it
spits me out through the teeth of time,
releasing four old captive syllables,
                        "I love you too!"—
           splitting the split
in the flow itself

Taking Space

Walking as I was
from waking
to sleep, I caught
this very moment, I mean
I found myself at this
particular angle of passing
the line itself,
and accidentally I found the path
leading straight into the sleeping state

stepping right off

into the nothing

in between

—where now? this must be
the famous moment of merging, the one
becomes the other, it's all taking place
and *not*
or nothing is like time, only opening, or

this
is a flower
emptying in space
in-
stantly, a change of air,
a certain thickening, a
wakening recoloring

I Found a Way

to be awake all the time.
It's so easy and
evident.
            I just start doing it
and instantly I know
everything—
            I say to myself,
"This is how you become everything!"

I turn to the guy sitting next to me—
and without hesitation I
show him how.
"Easy, isn't it?
Try it sometime."

In Brief

The body tiny, clearly
in its last moments, some-
body's going to be —poof!—

                              only a rainbow

Your Death

is numbered,

said the voice that came
from my two ears
as though beings were alive there.
Very matter of fact.
The phrase had a familiar ring
but something was off.
It could only mean
I'd made friends
with the contrary of my days
coming toward me now
with the best of intentions.

In Common

1

I was just standing around when the desire came over me
to get out of my body.
So how, in fact, do you
cut loose?
In a rush, a gust of wind
as if out of the earth itself
blows my body, part
by separate self-sensing part—
head, arms, internal organs—until
every last one turns transparent
as they rip away
integrating with air

2

Standing there, just being with
my friend Christine,
our arms stretched wide
to mirror each other open
until the bodies themselves touch
virtually, truly sensing
a nearing vanishing point,
clarifying the wish to merge
by letting the light
show through, and each
go all the way
to each other's other
side, far over

3

Only the last-ditch denominator, a question
left standing
between exist-
able residues, what now
in what remains?

Familiar Space

Dinner in the living room,
a party for twelve,
plates on the table, and some
soba noodles setting the pace.
A few people are already seated, and I'm moving
toward taking my place,
but there's a girl sitting in my usual spot....
I move on
toward a little bigger plate
reserved for you, and I reason
the best place for me is one chair away, so I can extend
my arm and touch you from the back and....

Stop. I've just realized something. A gift
of this occasion—it doesn't matter
where I sit.
                    By awareness alone
you can be in touch
with anybody, everybody
at the same time.
                    Right then
Barbara comes over, we start talking, I recount
the consequential events, she responds

                    "Oh *that*
                    is the act of
                    eso-grip"

—secret inner touch reaching
                    anywhere at once, any
                                        way you intend,
the actual physical experience of it,
                                        how it
        gets to you

How I Was Animated

1

I was an animated character
sitting back and
thinking and
gazing at things

and mostly sitting
right there
on the spot
and not getting involved
with things
no not at all

and my heart
got impatient with me
my red heart jumped
right out of me
and *bing!*

many hearts, and many many hearts
each one itself
traveling out and toward and reaching
to meet a thing all its own
and connecting, directly,
and getting straight into the matter of the thing

I knew instantly, animately, how right it is,
this way, whatever it is, this
heart breakout

2

I was getting back into
depressing thoughts
and all the old emotions that go along with them
and always and always the same question

how can I liberate these thoughts

—midway in the journey's un-
ending mental winding—like being
on a train curving round a
bend, confused
glimpse back
over the shoulder, seeing
what comes before
appears to be
coming from behind—
Wings!

are rising out of my back
one after the other
sensing their way from the
source spots on my re-
verse side, quick
flaps flying out into the sky, straight on,
turning up, and further up—lickety-
split, each lifts off
the wings
themselves take off and
vanish
behind me—dis-
appear the feeling itself,
set each
one free   *bing!*

A
Crack
in
the
Air

I saw it, instantly knew it, *this*
is the beginning of beginning.
Incredible I never got it till this moment—
the crack is vital
for the truly
not yet.

So much time is lost
not realizing
the simplest truth—

crrrraaack!

and light
finds its way through no matter what.
Like a promise—that the tiniest
aperture tearing through the air
is all it ever takes, a rip
no bigger than a twist in thought
cuts between
clinging to old whatevers
and the blinding abundance of
breaking light

7

(or 5)
plants
standing up
for different emotions.
One embodies my present emotional state,
a little depressed and angry.
So I turn my anger against this
apparent force pressing my spirits down,
and grab it by the throat
to pull it out by the roots!

But wait,
this can't be right.
Better to just
let the bastard grow....

And halfway through realizing I should leave it the hell alone
my anger disappears and, strange to say, I find myself
caring about a plant.
Instantly through the green something's showing in *the underlife*

—space opening, glowing—

Or is this *me?*
seeing things
as its possible life in hiding
suddenly mirrors....

Either way this is no ordinary house plant
waiting to be taken care of—
This one holds
its ground.

Cleaning

I was cleaning
and discarding things
—or you could call it dis-
regarding what wasn't
essential or, worse, could even be
harmful, because *not true.*
Meanwhile you were starting to get upset with me
for throwing things away.
You missed the point.
Things were hardly just things
but little weighted entities
bearing their own fields,
and I was there to strip them
down to the core.
I cut as I saw
according to the truth line—
clearly—aware
as much as I was
awake at my center,
the line of truth
is inside each
one, and every
thing self-
aligned there
through promises
to be

A Great Wheel Day

So many peacocks on the road I
had to stop to look,
yet none was opening
the iridescent fan.
I waited . . . hoping
at least to find a feather on the ground....

                                                 Not a one

to be found there.
I left, unable to shake the thought,
maybe they were holding back the
prized tail of eyes
because I asked a stupid question—

        "Do you live on an altar?"

"That's not so stupid," Susan slips in,
"The great Tibetan master Dudjom Rinpoche
            gives them free range across his altar."

Natural Offense

We were taking a little walk down the road
when off in the woods we caught sight of
a wolf and an elephant,
and more deeply in the field as if suddenly recalled,
a penguin.
And they were tracking us,
responsively open.
We didn't stop of course, just kept on
walking past the natural scene.
Then someone tore through the silence,
"Do you realize we're the
only ones
not surprised to see
elephant and wolf together,
not to mention the hint of a penguin?"
This brought us back
down to earth,
swept from ecological amnesia:
No doubt
they took offense.

I Heard They Caught the Blue Dragon

so I rushed out to see it
in the cold, dead place that looks
something like an aquarium

Standing there behind the seven
strangely unexcited watchers, I caught sight
of the notorious glass container,
an unfocusing five-foot rectangle brimming
with murky water

In the end it's hard to know more
than the pale medium shows—

short blue movements
and shining scales

Field Work

Stained
glass, highly
refined, tiny
round pieces, a
mosaic,
the light from behind
emerges

Strands of light shooting out from each glass piece

And each has a light baby.
Together they are called
Light Baby Bees.

I think I should protect them.
So I collect them in a basket.

And feed them
things found I sense are
good for their deep well-being.

But I never really know
if I'm doing the right thing after all.

What
should I do, how
in the world do you
take care of
light baby bees?

Portrait With Red Bird

I was telling you how dreaming I could hear
                                                        a certain noise

bwooom bwooom

    like a steamship, only faster,
                                                        so naturally I
looked around to see where it was coming from—

        A big bright red bird
was standing there on his two legs
pretending to be a human being.
        He opened his formidable beak
to show, inside, a human face
gazing out.

Riding in an open golf cart
connected to his own particular device for *sucking,*
      —vacuum cleaner ending in trumpet!—
he held the hose, aimed it and sucked air!

This he did in many directions, exercising his special gift—
      detecting heaviness.
At the first sign he'd track it down mercilessly and
suck without limitation, until all was utterly *out....*

Then it hit me:

maybe this could work on me!
He must have heard my silent request
because *without flinching*
he went straight into the upper right side of my head
(the place I know something's not quite right)
and sucked,

bwooom bwooom

letting the *thing* out!
And more of the same from part to part, from back to front,
until every last bit of heaviness emptied....

So what happened? you asked, *How did you feel?*
In truth I didn't recall any *significant* results —
nor do I now.
I felt obliged to fake an answer:
"It was so incredible—I felt so light after that."
And you replied, *"No kidding!"*

Still the mind—
back with the bird, red and sounding....

White Retriever

Out there on the screen
of my computer, looks like a little animal
—could be our white dog very tiny—
runs around and around, in and
out of unnoticeable spaces,
nearly unenterable cracks,
places so fine no one recalls them, where
it appears dreams
stray, as smoke, filigree, lost
strands along the way, slipping through
to nowhere,
                    yet
his gift is getting in
anywhere, sharply,
precisely seek and find
inside any hole
any dream. And so it happens

                                    I run
                                after him
                        trying to keep track
            he's so quick he gets sucked right
                            into the dream
                        crack, he loses me
                        or gets so far out
                        or in, I get con-
                            fused, whose
                retrieval, what bounding
                            line is being
                    crossed confounds me
        and my white dream trailing
        off, white dog running off

My White Dog

is walking along
and a black cat
goes beside him.

As it turns out, she
is his shadow.

And I
am he.

A Huge White Bear

on top of a great white mountain
standing high
on his hind legs
makes the gesture of receiving

and the light of the expanse above
comes all the way down
and down further
entering into him

and he turns
all the way
into the great
gold bear
up there on the huge
white mountain

The Place of Buttons

Here we are in the place of buttons—choices
of states to be in—and my sister is the one
among us who may choose.
With only one choice, she pushes the *white*:
the white button that puts you in the state of white.

In that very act she becomes the state itself,
she embodies it through and through.
Instantly a white bird flies toward her
and lands right next to her.
And two little white birds
mistake her head for their nest
and move right in.

I'm here keeping an eye on her,
terrified that any second the bird will fly away
and my sister will disappear too, because white,
by its nature, does not stay
for long.

And in the end I can't stand it, I can't help but reach out
to the bigger bird, to grasp it, to grab a hold, to hold it
down, yet all this desperate clinging is embarrassing
because I never escape knowing that it's useless,
for nothing can make it stay, nothing
can interfere with the nature of white.

Now I see you are here too, there
on the other side of the space,
so I ask you, take a picture of us all, make sure
to include the birds along with my sad awareness,
its way of being here in this fragile state,
and how I wake up inside it

This Beautiful Little Girl

in a shiny white dress
appears on stage in front of a crowd.

It's her debut.

Her tiny voice opens large into song,
uncannily binding in the ear.
It pulls me in, further in, and

as the spell unfolds I'm struck
by something strange—she's got
such huge breasts!
How cute, I'm thinking,
she's wearing falsies!
And little by little, behind the sweetness
in the voice, she's growing
older and
older, and the
song itself
waxes mediocre, even
boring, like inescapable pop radio.

And by the time the music ends
she's an ordinary grown-up young woman
satisfied with her own accomplishments.

Now it hits me, *This time-lapse siren's singing
sucks you into aging,* and
barely slipping out of its hold,
I never want to sing this song.

Blessèd Dolls

We're making
Jesus Christ
out of clay.
Three of us,
maybe four, and one
is teaching
how to make it come to life,
like a ritual:

Sit in a certain position,
make a circle, take clay out of the middle,
continuously say the mantra of Jesus Christ
without stopping
until it lives.

Q: What's it like?
A: I don't know, I didn't finish, I
woke up. And

it was later that day that we found the doll
in the basement, I mean the one from Chile we think of as
bringer
of everything
—his back loaded
with *one of each kind of thing.*

And so it is we decided to make dolls—
bearers of irreducible qualities
coming from all of us, so no one
stands out—and

sitting in a certain position —

Blessèd dolls.

Jesus Christ Is in the Room

and the top demon too,
who says to Jesus,
"Did you come first
or did I?"

Jesus answers, "Perhaps I
came first
because I didn't need anything"

and giving the sense
of his presence
as love moving slowly from one side of the room all the way
over
to the other, filling
us up

—"I'm so
happy to be here" is all
I can say to him.

Blue

CHAPTER ONE: *I Was a Giant Man*

Bright blue down jacket on my back.

And my true Teacher, kindly working on me, his hands
reaching down under me to take hold fully,
for all his mastery still has to struggle
because I'm so big.

People have me figured for a terrorist,
and now they were coming after me. I ran,
grew more desperate with every falling foot,

                                    and somewhere
in the world cut through

                I saw her, this little girl, I
                    felt compelled, I
                                    took her hostage.
                        Time
                and time again
            I realize
the danger is long since over, and still
I drag her along with me.

            You can't see her, she's gone inside,
                invisible against the other sky.

This big hall is full of fakes,
an endless supply of evangelists.
One after the other they come up front
auditioning for heaven, competing
for *your* spiritual dollars. They speak
bull, they shout and scream and sputter
and the people echo and take the fall
at their holy feet.   *I want to vomit.*

Then it hits me. These are my guys.
Unmistakable simple direct manifestations of actual acts of
dishonesty long forgotten
bearing their fruit before my eyes.
What in God's name have I done?

One runs up, his hour come round at last,
wearing this disgusting baby blue
vinyl jacket, emanation
of ultra-loathing, and starts preaching
with fine inspiration the purest trash of the universe, oh
regurgitate and get it over with.
            Last straw.   I take off running
                down the middle dead center
and knock him down to stop him dead
in the crush of the crowd.
                        *[My hope is what they'll take me for
                            is just one more fan in heat.]*

            But on his heels another, and another
                and louder yet another—

                *evangelical actions innumerable,
                rhetorical flourish imponderable—*

is there no end to it, wild rivals of the blue yonder,
            air thinning, face   turning...
                dying to be saved

They Kidnapped Me

to correct
my behavior.

Then yet another
came and took me
for something
better.

Limited Communication

An angel came to me.
I started to write down
how he is, what he's saying,
and right in the middle here I noticed that
I would no sooner write it down than
things got old
—not ancient, but the faded, useless kind of old.
The angel was sort of laughing,
so I insisted on continuing the writing,

                                              but now
the angel was becoming *ordinary.*
Oops! This is worse than useless. Better give it up.

Therefore this communication

                    ends here.

Sitting on Thin Glass

or a massive contact lens
iridescent
and collecting dew along the base

—This is a thing so
transparently fragile
I'm scared stiff I'll break
clear through

Whereupon a voice delivers

Not grave!
You're up in the air

I relax into the instant realization

I'm floating

while down on the ground
the poet Stein gazes up
stunned,
left hand lifted,
gently reaching,
releasing
ichthyoidal hooked-throat sounds

oolk oolk oolk

fishing the air to track me

G. Says He Knows How to Catch Time

                                        which is falling fast
                        from the tall building.

No one believes him but me.

For his part he's totally confident,
explaining that he'll use Manhattan,
which is three times the size of the falling time,
to catch it.

Just before it hits the ground
he indeed stops it.

It didn't even touch Manhattan.

At the same time I start to tell my dream
right here inside the dream.

"At last! The first in three months!" he says.
I get mad and say, "I'm not
telling you, period."

True Tangerines

A great mountain of tangerines
deliciously right there in front of me
and I'm dying to buy some!

"I'll need a *bunch* to satisfy this craving," I think as I lurch
at the blissful mound, one foot
halfway inside the luscious site

                        —but, my luck!—
                        not a soul in sight to sell 'em.

Just some guy's up there talking, or maybe lecturing, or
it's a new kind of game
played with an audience of avid listeners.
Now I get it, this is the leader,
and he's searching for *the truth* as he talks.
Each time a piece of truth comes through he
throws a tangerine at the audience,
always in exactly the *right direction*—
arresting action that flushes out the truth yet
further determines it.
At a certain point he brings out his invention:
        an organ-like machine with protuberant keys
        functioning as knobs that make no sound.
To play it you insert
each newly discovered truth
for the I-Ching shuffle of self-randomizing specificity
    settling
        the truth of the moment

              —temporary, still
                 utterly defining

                   just as it is
                   to itself

                            this very point
    in time, tasting of tangerine

Virtual Relations

FIRST CHAPTER: *Relating Details*

I killed an old lady.
So I had to go looking
for a place to get rid of her.
When none turned up, I had no choice
but to make a carrot cake out of her body—
huge, as cakes go.
Next came the problem of where to hide it,
and I resorted to walking around school, cake-in-hand.
People all but swarmed, saying,
"Wow, that sure looks good!"
pulling any trick to get a taste,
sticking a finger in here and there.

So when no one was looking I put it down
on the floor in front of the ladies' room,
hoping someone would step on it.
Bingo! An excuse to snatch it up and
ward off the pressing crowd with
"Injured cake—Please don't eat!"
I ran into the bathroom, threw it in the toilet, and flushed.

Meanwhile the police came looking for the missing woman.
I was worried about the cake platter—
Japanese police are so precise, even a hair will give you away—
so I wiped it clean, while trying hard to remember,
who was this old lady? No luck there.

Everybody's relative, someone said.   (Is that the expression?
                              I wonder if this is the Buddhist translation
                       of Einstein's view about absolutely everything.)

So who killed who? For all I know
she was already dead when I found her.
Then a related thought blew across my mind:
            Maybe, in the end, it was me,
            ready at last to be killed off

OTHER CHAPTER: *Unrelated Expression*

Incredible sensation! O my God!
Heart bursting into tears,
a fast flood erupting
right out in front of me!

I'm being flushed!

Whole body blown through, spent, then hollowed out, the

coolness of the wind

rushing through my channels

like crying and laughing at once
in the torrentially empty heart

livingly vast, spatially mortal

unbearably wanting it to last, knowing
any second it ends
in whiteout,

my blackout
dawns on me

Judging by Appearances

For the umpteenth time I was having this dream
in my dream. Of course I thought the obvious:

This is reality.

It took everything I had to perform the simple act
   of remembering
      at which the words leapt out of me:

> *I've stopped judging people*
> *by their appearance.*
> *I see them with different eyes now.*

As I was telling this experience and used the phrase
"impossible now to simply judge" you
immediately turned suspicious.

So I took you to a high place
where we could gaze upon the many
streaming into a place of dance.

I shifted focus.
Like switching eyes.
One person in the crowd had luminescence,
while the others just clouded out.

True judgment I see is assessing the pressure on the space
to allow communication.
"And this person," I said, "I judge
not by appearance but
force of glowing."

Real Feast

I was running
after myself.
Was running from
myself.
Not long after
I caught myself.
Got caught.
Right away I started
eating myself.
Then I noticed a guy there
next to me,
so I offered him a plateful,
a simple dish
with some jellied blood on it.
He turned up his nose
and flatly refused.
No matter. Nothing
to be offended about.
It's an offering —*who*
enjoys it isn't the point.
I accept the feast.
Down to the last morsel.

It's good, at long last,
to be accepted. To accept.
Naturally.

Meet Me in the Sky

1

This flying says it for me.
I mean I want to be known
by what it shows,
how I angle my wings,
the lift of the feather
against the air, the look
that blows across my face,
body turning out
of itself, tellingly.
If you want to know me,
just keep watching
for a space of time.

2

It takes me back
to the unrecallable place.
Someone in school is seeking me out—
math teacher, *sake* on his breath,
my childish name like a feather
beating the air

Chi-bu, Chi-bu

This is me, this is me

—I carry on in refrain—

straighten up and fly right

As if my stranger's song is waiting to say, *Come,*
come with me, the way I am.
turn your attention to the sky
that lets tell.

Spiral Trees

or

How to Interpret a Chinese Movie

Just the two of us here together, outside, our eyes
pinned to this Chinese movie. Look again—
are we at the edge of a painting
stunning our world into classic status?
Mist. Waterscape. Sumi. Possible
mountain there, can't quite see
through all this haze—yet
clearly the whole scene lives as one being.

Close in to the given space and
let your attention embrace any part
of its body—see! direct contact
wakes it up,
fingers the part to unfold, flowering
disclosure of another life
reverberant
all over the whole held view
sounding the system further alive:

Spiral trees
spiral out
Yet other spiraling
trees all around

And water, water
everywhere,
middling fold upon fold,
focusing forms
a little isolated land—

And on this intentional island
startled things happen
by sheer force of attending, and I

can only say, "Isn't it all amazing?"
"Yes," you return, "but I don't like this
pretentious narration."
"You're jaded!" I start to say when

suddenly on the lower left side of the scene
            the **Start** button appears. I click it and
                  A word surfaces

                  Oki Oki

            (could be Japanese)

And right away you contribute a philosophical reading.
"That's interesting," I say, "but totally wrong!"
All it really wants to say is:

            This sound itself is happy.

The movie moves on resoundingly
as the happy people walk around, one
by one releasing the given
yet utterly particular intoned
happiness emission —
                  being
            one's own
      willing island, *Oki Oki!*

Cooking with Earth

All manner of things
from the Earth, and I
thought I was cooking
with all of them.
Right away I was moving
them around in
intricately particular forms,
start to . . . *not* mix but
awaseru—I mean
let them meet—
gently, adjusting
and positioning
each one
so to get to know
each other,
and not just one but all
must meet, right
place, right
time, right touch
in the disposition
that each retain
its own form,
character, and taste
while taking on the flavor of
other things of the Earth
awakened in the contact,
hikidasu—I mean
to extract the essence—
that in this way you may create
the Universe at large
and all manner of things within it
as their very selves, favoring
being together

The Almond Tree

I'm walking and
you're walking—you
who are there be-
hind me—and

looking down at my legs you say,
There goes an almond tree!

This is language
self-secreting
like its own place
in the woods
we know
only together.

No sooner is it said when
we are directly intro-
duced to the

forest

the very place
I too am
now looking upon

the almond tree

even as we are,
you and I, walking
behind

Invisible Tree

Out walking with my teacher, a tree
almost closing in behind, just known
by what it lets fall
on the path before us —
                              leaves, twigs, acorns,
unrecognized seeding things
catching attention —
                    how something falls to
              land and scatters up again, slows
         from waving leaf into coloring air, each
      curve holding its space —

And all the while he is right there, somehow silently
instructing me, helping see, everything equally, see each
flashing thing to the quick, watch it
quiver its split-second way into the view,
rise with a thing to the horizon of its world
spreading before, way before, even long before, our walking —

Being out here. One walking moment as true as the next.
Swept along and passed through, nothing to hold to, no
urge to.
His showing. Slightly smiling. Presence of tree.

Word Expanse

1

This place is filled with words.
In the air, everywhere,
and it's physical.
                              The room is full.
The words themselves glow,
expand—
                    The view
is stunning—
                    and each word
is trying to find itself, reaching out
for its true place, and
at the same time all the words everywhere in the space are
moving toward realization,

                              then all of a sudden
clicking into place—
                              one by one
                    they settle
          on their spot
where they belong

          appearing to say

Words enjoy their primordial state

2

I was so sure I knew
this is what you do
as a poet.
I mentioned it to you, and you were so glad
that I understood.... And

all the endless night long I tried to remember this by
telling the dream, over and over, in new ways.
And the expert Dr. Cats was running out with a bad foot
while I was trying to *say* it, without using a Tibetan word
for the primordial state, but he never understood.
So three syllables leapt out of my mouth

héd-e-wa

—a sudden shock
to wake up in,

or perhaps it's a Tibetan squirrel-like being—

and he said, "Oh,
you must mean the Tibetan squirrel-like being...."
"No!!!" But he was gone. Not interested.

Still in deep with telling the dream to remember it and
see it inside certain possible perspectives, I knew I had to
address different people in different ways, all night long,
yet in the end it got too complicated,
and turning to our local philosopher, Chuck,
he (or maybe I) said,
"It's too dogmatic."
That is, a *square* state of mind.

It's more than sad for someone in my skin
—a witness
to the secret of words—
that despite these struggles of the night
I'm still unable to
pass it on....

Excavation

This is delicate work.
Now, after digging down
into the ground, the final stage at long last,
and the charge has lifted to the air we breathe—

Be aware

At all cost avoid trespassing onto the core substance
so like liquid emerald.

And there's an imperative:

you don't talk while doing this work.

But it's frustrating: my companions
are out of focus—they chatter, they joke,
insist on doing everything their own way.
They have no idea what must be done.

This is the moment of birth itself—
no time, no space left for
mere talk, and I fear

It is right on the verge
of disappearing—

the green glow in the ground calling to the surface,
recalling

KOTODAMA

the syllable spirits

declaring this site *open*

—*words* breaching ground each god breaks through in—

back alive!

Afterwords

Millennial Name

Year 2000. Until now
I thought my birth name *Chie* meant *a thousand pictures*.
But as the century grinds to a halt
there's a bug —
                          it takes my pictures along with it
back to the beginning.
Zero zero. One by one
I'm in a name/death struggle to live up to the promise
of original meaning:
                          produce the many, the greater
number born in picture
upon picture
in an actual piece.
Work my way up to what it says I am.

Until then I'm at zero point figuration.
I feel naked,
stripped of everything I thought
given.

Yet there's something exciting about it—
like a whole history cleared out in the flick of a glitch.
Back to the origin. Nothing left
but being
brand new.

Drawings

a note on visual time

THE THIRTEEN DRAWINGS are placed throughout *Ainu Dreams* according to "temporal field" rather than either established pattern or specific reference. They are not connected directly with buun's dreams, but they were composed contemporaneously with the poems. The origin of the drawings is always spontaneous, without "subject" or "object," and I think of them as essentially free and unpredetermined, coming from a "state of listening attention" and a "discipline of release." Like dreams they come in multitudes, with no regularity and with many nuances of coherence.

To me they are neither figurative nor abstract but *configurative,* which is liminal to both. That is, figures come and go, catching attention with a will of their own, letting it go without notice, without formal commitment. Somehow they are animate, animating, self-animated. They trace their own time, as if keeping a story hidden. As a record they are barely there. Or what's there is a trail: traces of their time, bare awarenesses.

These particular drawings were chosen—from the many hundreds in my notebooks—in a collaborative effort by buun and myself, as elements of the book's *timed space,* according to a sense of *interval and absence.* This relates in our minds to the Japanese notion of *ma* [see ideogram on page one], a *natural distance or time-space between.* Any visual incursion in the flow of text creates its own special time that carries over to the "area" around nearby poems. They show time as something created. So the drawings are not illustrations but neighbors. Likeness draws them close.

Like neighbors, like poems, the drawings are *there* even as the dreams themselves aren't quite—except as particularly engaged through reading, indeed *called* to the site. Yet the drawings seem to be just passing through the land of text, and in the process many species of time become palpable. Perhaps they obliquely instruct in the nature of "poetic presence"—that it too but flashes into view and is gone before the mind gets a grip. Invited guests that sometimes show.

The sense of *ma* in ancient times was focused in terms of specific attractive force—an invitation to the *kami* (loosely defined, "space-time gods") to inhabit a defined temporal-spatial location. Our interest could be characterized more modestly as spirited attention alighting within points charged with emptiness. Presence of the dream, barely.

buun had a strong hand in the organization of the book, and our sense of structure was what emerged from the effort to create a neighborhood. In such a process one becomes aware of fields of intentionality, overlapping and resonating. The drawings, the poems, the dreams—they're like us, *bounding* with, against and across what is near. Intentional activity within limitation. Yet always with a sense of permission, which arises naturally in a good neighborhood.

The process of placement of poems and drawings provided its own instruction in the nature of collaboration—an art that includes offering each other timely breathing space between emerging intensities. *Ma*, the between, allows the listening that in turn prepares a work to find its zero point. Point?—well, call it the *source* beyond understanding. There, any contact discharges the itch to interpret what is happening, or to otherwise get in the way.

Oneiropoeia

telling tales on dreaming

EVERYONE DREAMS—we think. But what do we really know? Nothing is more tantalizing than the dream as an "object" of thought, because it won't stay still. It won't even stay *there*. Its nature as *object* seems to end up challenging the nature of objects. When you recall a dream, it may be like going to meet an ancient friend rumored to have grown *more animate* by means of his own unstable agenda. You have to give up your own agenda just to track him. You need unwavering clarity to see through his ruses. The greatest disadvantage in taking hold of him is the fact that you think you know him. The only real hope is committed ignorance. Then the lightning speed of apprehension may find a crack—the essential crack—to flash through... *just in time.* Well in advance of the thunderclap that will drive him back into hiding.

If everyone dreams, not everyone *claims* to dream, indeed some claim never to dream. Perhaps what goes on in the dream state for these "non-dreamers" doesn't correspond to what mind habitually registers as dream. Or they have a rational frame that is unfriendly to dreams. Or they have been misled by an ordinary sense of the extraordinary. People tend to tell the dreams that make good stories, and stay away from those that remain alien to storytelling. Yet to approach dreams for their story value alone impoverishes them, gives them the message that their unlimited non-narrative states of telling are not welcome in the land of language. So there are endangered species in the dream world too. Delicate ones, shy ones, variously insubstantial, ever on the verge of extinction through mere understanding. Someone needs to boldly go where no storyteller has dared. ...To let dreaming tell itself, to make itself up as it goes, to perform its uncertain limp and inevitable disjunctive leaps—to step out beyond the memorable. "I can't remember my dream" is perhaps the most common report. But what if memory is only one of the roads in? Or if what one needs is an attractor that calls the dream out into its further life?

THE POEM is well equipped to apply for the job. To really qualify, however, the poem may need to suspend certain of its own merely familiar modes of self-awareness. It may need to stand exposed to its own cracks. To get close to its own impossibility (which may run counter to its "creative program"). If one of the problems of telling dreams is that they are to some very large degree bent upon failure—committed to eluding report and subsequent incorporation in the interpreted world—then a poetry that has forsaken aspiration may attract the dream into a mutually acceptable environment. Some place not too well lit. Craggy, lush, internally spacious, intermittently empty, perilous, falling out of balance, rushing beyond judgment, still, declared open.

All/none of the above. But it doesn't hurt to tilt our thought. Dream's enemy is certainty, self-assuredness, style, skill, mastery. It seeks a free and easy dance partner capable of reserving a power of all possible dances, yet a power understood by no one. All cultures welcome, all forbidden without notice. And times ... time itself wearing the masks, the histories, personal stories, soap operas, tabloid epics with the attention span of a praying mantis—prophetic, lunching on mates, eating in tongues. But we are slipping out of our mode here. Truly to speak of dreams is to dream in speaking. One entrains to the wild.

WE BECOME WHAT WE BEHOLD, says Blake, and if we may put words in his *muthos:*
Faced with the nightmare of history, he slammed the translation vehicle of Prophetic Poetry into reverse, drove "English, the rough basement" backwards through the terror of Sleep toward the possibility of **waking outside,** *inside the Illuminated Book. He proved the working power, like an action on the blacksmith's anvil or "printing in the infernal method, by corrosives."* **Proving** *—homeopathically—the "test by experience" is performed in oneself, like seeking its transformative like, begetting its kind "made new"—* **in telling.**

This is the oneiropoeic principle that

by poesis speaking dreams direct

—*performs the work at the limen of sleep, proposes the non-dual surface of dream-waking—something like a Klein Form[1] seamlessly accommodating unlimited disjunction, and lets loose a speaking— a prosopopoeia—of all absent possible selves alive and well on the verge of waking. Blake through.*

TELL ME YOUR DREAM, I say to her every morning. Poetry is waiting. Speaking from sleep is a liminal affair. Soft words. Swelling at the lips. They don't all fit through the aperture. Distention. They tear. What gets out rushes out. Flashes in the mind in sudden outline. Sheer paint, stalled colors, then bleed through. *Everything possible to be mumbled is an image of the dream.* Some of the beings in hiding make their way to the surface, push their way through the pout of utterance. Superficial profundity.

dream
surfaces

OBSTACLES TO ARTICULATION are the very objects of the dreamscape.

—The state of *showing through the speakable* is the exception.

—Yet when dream does make it past the guardians of the sayable, it's not that it now *becomes* language, but that it shows its other side *as language.*

DREAM IS LANGUAGE, and all attempts to understand language as necessarily different from dream impoverish both language and dream. Dream's refusal to speak points toward a truth of language, the "failure" of language to disclose. Poetry discloses the intentionality of this refusal/failure to disclose. And:

ONEIROPOEIA is the domain of poetic working that inhabits this strange area at the threshold of dreaming, including the impossibility felt to lie so fruitfully within

dream saying

A Common Axis

In order for the poem to become the surface of the dream it has to discover something like a common axis—an empty center that runs through the dream yet is located through the poem. The discovery of the axis of the dream, in fact, may only be possible through a correlative domain, a declared remove from the dream that creates a conscious reentry, crossing the threshold with an active tongue, a medium, a middle surface, a sublime liminality.

Sublime—a concept word too long on the lam—has always new force in the (al)chemical sense of *change of state toward the optimal*. Of course this correlative domain implies a discipline and may be psychological, therapeutic, somehow philosophical, variously artistic, including poetic or, most especially, *metapoetic*. The latter implies the possibility of any or all of the above at once, many intentional functions in a single act of making. More important, the encompassing metapoetic function consists in this: that the change of state toward the optimal involves a transformative power within language, its peculiarity of knowing. This knowing, at its most originary, the optimal itself, I no longer resist calling *lognosis*.

THE COMMON AXIS BETWEEN DREAM AND POESIS implies a *precarious balance*. As a person with a passion for working with natural stones in particular states of equilibrium —to see them in a state of showing more than *our* prejudice of gravity and *their* obvious element—I naturally point to a sort of analogue:

balanced stone, eloquently silent, tenuously showing secret depths

---

utter surface

Here superficial means profound.

For instance, deeply felt spoken meaning may enter the condition of language as it lifts off the skin—*tongued,* just as it sounds.

Staring at a precariously poised surface you entrain to your own depth, and work your way out, differently. One registers extremely improbable equipoise not mainly through the eyes but through the whole body, the body as organ of perception—organ of intervention.

One *reads* the balanced stone through an *axial sense*, the central axis of the body registering disturbance. Likewise: dream surfaces through an open axis, activating the whole of the dream body. Dream surfaces by coming into the body, and so, by way of incursion, discovering *its* body through *the* body—the common axis.

THE AXIAL FORCE runs invisibly through everything, holding appearance at a pitch of reversibility—poetry, *verse,* the turn upon the possible, precariously equiponderant upon impossibility, belongs in the nature of language to the root from which dream in its essential power arises. At bottom they are spoken from the same mouth. To serve the dream poetry offers its root nature. It bends forward in the wind, angling to speak in colors, multiples.

THE OTHER('S) SONG is always the other name for the "Ainu Dream." It carries the teaching of the dream, whose message begins: *the most intimate knowing is indistinguishable from the most "alien."* With a corollary: We are other to ourselves to the extent that we are not intimate with our source, in touch with the never-disconnected nature of essential cognition. To invoke the *collaborative* process of the work—labor that is always dual, dialogical, speaking for the truth of individual multiplicity—is to see its nature as nonseparable, and to turn back to the dream itself as inherently collaborative.

THE AINU[2]

Why? Why indeed. I am on the verge of making up a story: *The Ainu, a shamanic people of unknown origin still living in Hokkaido, are exemplars of the collaborative.* No doubt true. The simpler truth is I can't get them out of my mind. I know all too little about them, never met one, never studied the language. I have mainly read, many years ago, the astonishing epic poetry, sung mostly by women, in the translations of Donald L. Philippi, *Songs of Gods, Songs of Humans,* and listened to the haunting recordings of shamanic Ainu epic singers. They attract something in me that didn't know it was there to be attracted.

It seems the earth listens to itself through them.

But it would be fatuous to claim any "real" connection between our Ainu Dreams and the actual songs of the Ainu. We pay respect to their intimate connection to the power of dream, its power to haunt—homing, frequenting, settling in, staking ground in the mind. But the name *Ainu* has a currency all its own in our discourse. Gary Snyder has called attention, in the Foreword to Philippi's translations, to the Ainu term *iworu*, "field of force"—"a term that can mean biome, or territory, but has spirit-world implications." We might add, with resonances of Charles Olson's "composition by field," that the force field extends as far as the mind can hear. ("How is it far if you think it?"—Olson) The Ainu field has somehow crossed over into our oneiropoeic sensorium, or the Klein Form of that inner sensing has met itself out there face to face with the Ainu. This is the actual extension of the dream body, which in the end encompasses the poem that embodies the dream. Does the dream have an outside other than oneself?

RECITAL

The recital [récit] *is neither a story nor an allegory ... not a story that happened to others, but the soul's own story, its "spiritual romance," if you will, but personally lived: the soul can tell it only in the first person, "re-cite" it ... an Event of the soul ....*

Henry Corbin[3]

The tale [récit] *is not the narration of an event, but that event itself, the approach to that event, the place where that event is made to happen—an event which is yet to come and through whose power of attraction the tale can hope to come into being, too.*

Maurice Blanchot[4]

THE DREAM IS A RECITAL in any instance of utterance, clearly, a tale told under a "power of attraction" whose time is the space of its own possibility. But isn't it also always already a recital to itself in its aspect of knowing itself? I see myself in my dream by way of an always surprising species of reflection, a performance of myself (whom I do not always instantly recognize). To the extent that I am aware of dreaming while in a dream, I am—*I is*—performative[5], the very identity which is at once subject and object in reflection.

It is tempting to call dream the *reflective performative*—what *is itself in the very act of articulation* and *only knows itself thereby*. If it had its own grammar accounting for its specific verbal nature, it might be called the *performative reflexive*—the subject *becoming itself* in the act of *recognizing* the object *as* itself or as inseparable from itself. In dream we invent new grammars in every moment as an aspect of practicality—how we practice what we are in the performance of the telling underway. This is a strange way of speaking, perhaps, but speaking about dream eventually entrains to dreaming itself. The writing of Gaston Bachelard is such a case, which teaches that of which it speaks through the degree to which its "subject matter" (the "poetics of space" or "reverie") acquires a curious presence in his telling. An oneiropoeia is in performance—*en permanence*—throughout. Oneiropoeia—the poetics of dream recital—subjects matter to its virtual transubstantiation.

subject
_____

matters

In dream subject crosses the line to matter.
That I am thrown under myself matters.
I matter transubstantially.
Thrown down I substantiates.

Each utterance is axial as dream is axial

It stands in the free and open space of its own turning upon its occasion—and is therefore *amphibolous*, thrown to either side, the meaning as the sense of the field with all its self-divergence, the cast of a net *large*—enough to meet its actual occasion. The axial phrase can go either way, not out of indifference or programed malleability, but out of responsiveness to one's own root and its primordial ambivalence. This ambivalence is not merely the inevitable war that one has with oneself (one's selves), though perhaps that too; rather, it is the expression of one's radical realization of non-separability within oneself *despite* self-contradiction, despite life's confusing multiplicity.

The axial is a capacity of language as a capacity of mind.

Oneself thrown down, subjected to the "laws of grammar," reflector of the rejected object—so much the matter of dreaming:

I discover my own way out of the subjective trap transgressively, transjectively, through the recital, the telling. I am performed through an incursion of my own torsional possibility, what, by its turning, churning and torque within me, breaks me out through the strange otherness of dreaming telling. Strange to say.

Best said by another—and this is the secret collaborative truth of oneiropoeia. Dream as the loneliest performance is never truly alone, indeed radically exposes our lonely non-aloneness, our inevitable tangle with others by the very condition of languaging. Telling implies listening. Listening performs another, another's telling, and another telling of one's own.

THIS PERFORMATIVE LISTENING characterizes for me the discovery at the heart of *Ainu Dreams*. After many years of writing out of my own dreams, already a practice of the other, I came to see the non-separability of dream performance in and of itself. I love to listen through the dreams of other people, but it never occurred to me that the poem would follow me there, allow me to find it there. By what "right" does one write another's dream?

Listening deeply through another's telling, as if one were tuning into the dream itself, finds its own law, its *right of precession,* of motion of the axis of its *spin*. There is a legality of the given moment like the once only law in the wobble of a pivot when external force acts upon the axis. The torque of telling has a quality of transport, to "a land" of its own dimension, implying a language specific to another dimension, to which poetry is liminal.

The poem is aroused trans*verse*ly by the listening, is moved to mind the gap.

buun is one of several dreamers, "epic" in the oral poetry sense, I have had the good fortune to listen to and through. These are people who accept dream as instruction, not in the "predictive" sense but simply in the *dictive*—it tells, it's telling:

The event is a transmission. To hear it is to be instructed.

One does not necessarily think new thoughts although one may think differently; and it is not a matter of interpretation, particularly where that implies a system or principle (psychological, religious, philosophical, aesthetic); on the contrary, what we are pointing to here is outside the interpretative. One protects the delicate life of the dream by preserving it from interpretation, at least until it finds its openness of form, its permission to *be* through telling. Faced with dream recital, one *stands* otherwise than one has stood, by way of the wisdom of that other telling—like leaning into the recital, with the result that one experiences *one's own other axis*. Then the telling goes on in the further life of one's being there, in the way that one is.

IN MENTIONING EPIC DREAMERS I continue to pay homage to the Ainu, intrinsically unexampled tellers, as well as the people I have alluded to, certainly not invidiously or as any implied comparison between "oral" and "literate" cultures—this is not my issue. The modality here is an expression always of gratitude, a way of thanking them all for their willingness to tell, as though in "dream" more is at stake than private property. This is a "more" that implies a *property of the mind* (to borrow Robert Duncan's phrase) that would be diminished immeasurably by a sense of *private* (as in "privation"), but not by a sense of *intimate;* diminished too by a notion of *own* that does not include *other.* Oneiropoeia has its own species of aspiration, of breathing not so much upward as outward toward the optimal inter-bounding.

I live with and therefore within the dreams of these others. I have precise recall of so many of Susan Quasha's dreams that it's like having an alternative life to draw from—an intercarnation. Likewise the dreams of Charles Stein and Robert Kelly over something approaching three decades—dreams that have been and still are my teachers. Likewise Franz Kamin's—which I can hardly separate from his writing and his music, resounding in/out the Klein Form of his very non-ordinary reality. Dreams by Fatima Lacerda are like magically powered novels I have read, almost written. Carolee Schneemann's dreaming allows an imagination of erotic merging between dimensions, species that embrace through our awareness— but aren't we straining dream as limit and entering the oneiric liminal?

Initiations, transmissions—shared with these friends. And in this register I must mention the dreams of a teacher in yet another, more encompassing, sense, those of Choegyal Namkhai Norbu, whose dreams we have had the immeasurable good fortune to hear over the past thirteen years and which occupy the place of sacred text with resonance far beyond the scope of the present discourse. His presence is felt in many nuanced ways throughout the Ainu Dreams.

SO IT IS THAT THE SOURCE of these poems enjoys a lifelong emerging context that speaks both within and beyond "personal history." This source arose spontaneously when I heard buun telling her dreams (in English, infused with Japanese qualities), which moved me with the force of a poem but without the realization in language. I registered this "call" by writing "The Fool," and this created for me an inevitability of this work. What is most special about the kind of interaction between me as "poet" and buun as "dreamer" is the declaration of a shared responsibility in *cultivating* an oneiric and poetic space. (Declaration, in this specific sense, means affirming an intuited possibility and aiming to actualize it, yet preserving its virtuality, the reach of possibility; such a declaration is not simply a willful projection of a wish, but is grounded in what always already is true.) You could say that the space is *held in common*. There is a bond—a deeply held commitment—a continuous maintenance of mutual consent, retaining over time a certain power, in this case some four years.

In the process of working with buun, I had a new perspective on the way both dream and poem are self-educating in the space of reflection. Her first language is Japanese and she had little experience of poetry (especially in English, although she has read widely and complexly in both languages); yet her participation in the poem was precisely inspired—particularly at the level of rectification, as the interruptive voice of the rights of the dream, and, too, as the continuous presence of the critical corrective that stays within the flow and rhythmus of poetic unfolding. It was like having the gift of a mind in reserve. Incursion was always there waiting to happen. Yet the poem's own intelligence, arising somewhere in the between, grew in unpredictable clarity, sure of its selfless self.

Sometimes when the poem hit an impasse, it knew to tell me to press her to remember what she said she couldn't, and then she did—memory as response to request. When we differed on the rightness of particular phrasing, I almost always yielded—discarding all favorites in favor of the dream's discriminating awareness. Yet there were instances of the poem's supplying something like a reverse corrective, in which she came to see her dream for the first time through the poem, or its way of informing her awareness changed, as it were, *along a poetic line.* This, frankly, astonished us both. *Poetic powers* were hardly "metaphoric," except in the sense of *the bearer of change.*

There were not *no* boundaries—there were and are always already *only* boundaries, what Blake called *the bounding line,* the living changing outline of anything that breathes. To be sure, no boundary escaped the willing change of *bounding*—the inter-bounding and bonding of common domains, to which dream is the intimate inter/intrapersonal access. And poetry is the language of the limen.

In its own time, of its undertime, at play on the surface of the dream, where

$$\frac{\text{time itself}}{\text{surfaces}}$$

as

$$\frac{\text{one's}}{\text{own outside}}$$

NOTES

[1] "Klein Form" would be the more abstract level of the Klein Bottle or, topologically, a one-sided three-dimensional surface having no inside or outside because all sides are continuous with all other sides.

[2] (University of Princeton Press and University of Tokyo Press: 1979.) Philippi's book has been our principal source of information on the Ainu, an indigenous shamanic people of undetermined (non-Japanese) origin now concentrated mostly in Hokkaido. Their situation in many ways parallels that of Native Americans and other indigenous peoples who have suffered a long history of oppression, exploitation and discrimination under a dominant alien culture. Preservation of Ainu culture—language, dance, poetry, etc—is an active concern, reporting some gains in recent years. See the Ainu Museum on the World Wide Web from Shiraoi, Hokkaido for more information. They report: "Ainu" means "human." The Ainu people regard things useful to them or beyond their control as "kamuy" (gods). In daily life, they pray to and perform various ceremonies for the gods. These gods include: "nature" gods, such as of fire, water, wind and thunder; "animal" gods, such as of bears, foxes, spotted owls and rampuse; "plant" gods, such as of aconite, mushroom and mugwort; "object" gods, such as of boats and pots; and gods which protect houses, gods of mountains and gods of lakes. The word "Ainu" refers to the opposite of these gods.

[3] *Avicenna and the Visionary Recital,* transl. Willard Trask, Bollingen Series LXVI: 1960.[in French, 1954].

[4] "The Song of the Siren," transl. Lydia Davis, *The Station Hill Blanchot Reader: Fiction and Literary Essays* (Barrytown. Ltd./Station Hill: 1999) [in French, 1959].

[5] *Performative* in this usage is the term created by the philosopher J.L. Austin to point to utterances that literally perform the action of which they speak: e.g., I promise, I wish, I accuse, I name, etc.—actions performed in the very saying (as opposed to referring to a secondary object). Such verbal actions close the gap between word and meaning, but performative utterances can only do their work in the specific contexts that call them forth: *performative language is always site/occasion-specific and concrete.*

Tamashi

TAMASHI, the native Japanese word for *spirit*, is contrasted by D.T.
Suzuki with the Chinese word for spirit, *Jing Shen* [pronounced *Sei
Shin* as the loan word in Japanese]. The latter is distinguished from
the material and therefore projects a duality in the distinction "spirit".
But the Japanese word suggests a sense of spirit that is finally non-
separable from the material—not without a certain tension between
the material and the spiritual, yet never without the possibility of an
embrace between them. What is known as "spirit" is itself almost
something you could hold in the palm of your hand. *Tama*—residu-
ally sounds the roundness of a ball, sphere, jewel, something pre-
cious and immediate to the senses. *Kotodama*—literally "Word Spirit"
[*dama* = *tama*]—brings spirit into words—syllables spoken or writ-
ten—open to "Excavation" by way of the ear—entitative spirit being
liminal to material and non-material and always coming alive again
in the liminally sayable.

TAMASHI

as she saw half waking

grab a hold

of any part of the universe

opening itself in the middle

POMEGRANATE

the view from the split

purpura and fleshy

squeezing in spirited being inhabitant

inwardly in touch breaking in through

to all and else

Biographical Note

George Quasha's work in poetry in recent years—following *Amanita's Hymnal, Somapoetics,* and *Giving the Lily Back Her Hands*—has continued in several strands: the "axial" poems (a selection of which comprises *In No Time*), the "oneirica" (including *Ainu Dreams*), and an open modality working with both the "somapoetic" and axial principles (*The Preverbs of Tell— News Torqued from Undertime*). The axial principle extends across mediums to visual and sound work—sound performance, drawings, stone works, installation and video.

His ongoing collaborations with Charles Stein and Gary Hill, begun in the 1970s, include sound poetry (e.g., *Tale Enclosure,* a Gary Hill single-channel video), text and on-site development of the installation *Disturbance (among the jars)* at the Centre Georges Pompidou in Paris, various kinds of writing and live performances, the latter extending his over twenty years of performance and dialogical work with Charles Stein. Also with Charles Stein he has co-authored many works, including three recent books in a series, *Gary Hill's Projective Installations 1-3: Hand Heard / liminal objects, Tall Ships,* and *Viewer.*

He has edited several poetry anthologies including *America a Prophecy* (with Jerome Rothenberg), *Open Poetry* (with Ron Gross), and *Active Anthology* (with Susan Quasha); the journal *Stony Brook* (with Roger Guedalla); and, recently, *The Station Hill Blanchot Reader.*

He received an NEA Fellowship in poetry. In 1978, after teaching many years (SUNY Stony Brook, Bard College, Naropa Institute, and The New School for Social Research), he and Susan Quasha, with whom he continues to work and collaborate, founded Station Hill Press. In recent years they have enjoyed a creative partnership with Chie (buun) Hasegawa in Barrytown, New York where they live.

Chie (buun) Hasegawa's own work has been principally as artist working with natural materials—stones, discovered objects—in ways that elude definition, yet witness a coherent world in miniature, from which her dreams bring further news.

Designed and typeset by George Quasha
with the help of buun and Susan Quasha.
The text is set in ɪᴛᴄ Stone Informal with Centaur titling.
Cover design and photo collaboration are by buun, George
Quasha and Susan Quasha, based on an idea by buun.
The cover is set in Calligraphic 421, Baker Signet,
ɪᴛᴄ Novarese and ɪᴛᴄ Stone Informal.
The book is printed on acid-free paper by BookMart press.